A History
Hope Baptist Churc

'And they continued steadfastly in
and fellowship and in breaking of bread and prayers'.

Acts 2.42

Dedication

This book is dedicated to the memory
of the author's father and mother, Mr. & Mrs. W.D. Osborne.
They were totally devoted to Hope Chapel and were very active
in its affairs for many years.
Elected a deacon in 1923, W.D. Osborne served as Assistant
Secretary, Treasurer and then as Church Secretary (1947-71).
He was Superintendent of the Band of Hope,
a Sunday School teacher and also a local preacher.
Mrs. Osborne was leader of the Sisterhood from its formation
in 1926 until her death in 1954. She was also well-known
as the teacher of an extremely large and very successful
Sunday School Class.

It is also dedicated to my wife Sylvia. It was at Hope
that I first met her and, after 42 gloriously happy years of
married life, it was at Hope that her funeral took place,
over 12 years ago.

*   *   *

I should like to express grateful thanks to Miss Teresa Fisher
for typing and preparing a floppy disc containing material covering
the history of Hope from 1982 onwards.

The colour cover photographs by courtesy of Reverend Stephen Jackson

© Dr. Graham O. Osborne

First published in October 2006

All rights reserved

The right of Dr. Graham O. Osborne to be identified
as author of this work has been asserted by him
in accordance with the
Copyright, Designs and Patents Act, 1993.

ISBN 1 905967 00 4

Published in the U.K. by
Old Bakehouse Publications
Church Street,
Abertillery, Gwent NP13 1EA
Telephone: 01495 212600 Fax: 01495 216222
Email: oldbakehouseprint@btopenworld.com
Website: www.oldbakehouseprint.co.uk

Made and printed in the UK
by J.R. Davies (Printers) Ltd.

All rights reserved.
No part of this publication may be reproduced, stored in a retrieval
system, or transmitted in any form or by any means, electronic,
mechanical, photocopying, recording or otherwise, without
the prior permission of the author and/or publishers.
For the avoidance of doubt, this includes reproduction of any
image in this book on an internet site.

British Library Cataloguing in Publication Data: a catalogue
record for this book is available from the British Library.

INDEX

FOREWORD   By Rev. Stephen Jackson (Pastor)

INTRODUCTION   By Graham O. Osborne (Dr.)

HISTORY OF HOPE CHURCH: - 1882-1982

HISTORY OF HOPE CHURCH: - 1982-2006

APPENDIX

PART 1
List of Ministers of Hope Church.

PART 2
Members of Hope Church who have entered the
Ministry and/or have carried out Missionary
Work Abroad.

PART 3
Hope Sunday School Building.

PART 4
The Church Covenant and Statement of Faith.

POSTSCRIPT

FOREWORD

In seeking to cope with the demands of the present and the absorbing passions for our futures, we are so often in very real danger of forgetting how vitally important our pasts are. All our pasts lay down something for our futures. Therefore, in order to lay down good foundations for that which is to come we must of necessity take stock of all the varied experiences of those who have journeyed before us.

Like so many Church congregations, the succeeding generations of believers here at Hope have sought to worship, work and witness against an ever-changing society that surrounds them. Much of what happens within the life of the local church to some extent can be reflected in one way or another in the records that they keep.

Dr. Graham Osborne is well placed to this task of researching and collating such information from the records of this congregation's life and times. His background as a Senior Lecturer and Scientist, coupled with his many ventures into research and authorship have been further enhanced on this occasion with his very close family ties with Hope Baptist Church, Crosskeys.

At this time of celebration for us here at Hope with the arrival of our 125th Anniversary, we are most grateful for Dr. Osborne's efforts to present a record of our past. We lay it on record that his many hours of research and presentation in the form of this book is most thankfully received by us all here. We would like to think that the book would receive a wider readership, especially maybe from one-time members and friends of the church. It may be that it will cause you to return should you not be involved with any other congregation. The present day people of Hope are as passionate about the building as they are about the One who is at the very heart of its purpose and presence. We absolutely assure you of the warmest of welcomes today as our predecessors sought to express in their time.

I am therefore delighted to commend this account to you and in doing so give thanks to God for all His blessings on this company of believers throughout the years so far.

Stephen Jackson (Pastor)
The Manse
14 Carlton Terrace
Crosskeys
Gwent. NP11 7BU

A HISTORY OF HOPE BAPTIST CHURCH, CROSSKEYS

By

Graham O. Osborne

INTRODUCTION

The foundation stone of 'Hope' was laid on 4th March 1880, and after the church was finally completed and furnished, opening services were held on 18th February 1882 and on the next three Sundays.

Following the completion of the Centenary Celebrations in March 1982, a Centenary History of the Church was published (in 1985). This work has recently been brought up to date with an addendum covering the period 1982-2005. In the present volume the original Centenary History is reproduced, together with the addendum. This covers 123 years of Hope's history. Hope will celebrate its 125th anniversary in 2007 and the present work has been compiled with this in mind.

It is hoped that this volume will be of interest not only to the Church Members but to a wider public, especially to those still living in the area, who down the years, have had connections with Hope Church.

Introduction

(a)   The Ancestry of Hope

Despite the fascinating report by Joshua Thomas (the first historian of the Baptist cause in Wales) that Baptists were meeting together in the remote Olchon valley (in the Black Mountains) as early as 1633, the fact is that the very earliest history of the Baptist denomination in Wales remains unknown.[1] However, there is no doubt that Gwent was the cradle of Welsh Protestant Nonconformity. The first Welsh Nonconformist Church was that established by William Wroth (formerly Rector of Llanvaches) at Llanvaches in 1639 and a branch of this church was established at Penmaen, in the parish of Mynyddislwyn later on in the same year. But it is by no means clear whether any Baptists were present in this *'gathered'* church.[2][3]

What is known is that by 1652, John Miles, a native of Newtown in Herefordshire and a soldier or chaplain in Cromwell's Parliamentary Army, had founded five Baptist churches in south Wales. The first church was founded at Ilston, near Swansea, in 1649. Churches were established in rapid succession at Hay-on-Wye, at Llanharan (near Llantrisant), at Carmarthen and finally, in 1652, at Abergavenny (Llanwenarth). An Association was then formed.

Times must soon have become difficult for these infant churches, for from 1660-1688 considerable restrictions were often placed on the right of Nonconformists to worship in public. Their civic rights were curtailed and they were sometimes also subjected to actual persecution. But in 1689 the religious climate changed and with the passing of an Act of Toleration it again became possible for Nonconformist churches to meet and worship openly. In this year the six existing Welsh Baptist Churches decided to join with the London Baptist Association and amongst the six are the names of four of the five churches founded by John Miles. The Carmarthen church seems to have disappeared in the difficult years after 1660 but two new churches had been founded during this time. One was at Rhydwilym (in West Wales). A second church was also established at Abergavenny; this second *'open-communion'* church differed from the churches founded by Miles which were all *'close communion'*.

Throughout the eighteenth century the total number of Baptists in south Wales appears to have increased only slowly. It should be remembered that in 1750 most of the Welsh Valleys were still thinly populated rural backwaters. Only in the iron-manufacturing towns of Merthyr Tydfil and Blaenavon had there been any appreciable population growth and mass industrialisation was yet to come. The principal places of worship were a few Anglican churches. These served enormous but sparsely peopled parishes whose boundaries had remained virtually unchanged since the Middle Ages. The churches, built for the occupants of the widely dispersed hill farms of these enormous parishes were often sited on hilltops (e.g. Mynyddislwyn). Later on this proved to be a disadvantage.

The few, early Baptist Churches also drew their membership from wide areas. Attendance involved much travelling and must have been very difficult, especially in winter, so branch churches were soon being set up. The Abergavenny (Llanwenarth) church founded a branch at Blaenau Gwent quite early on and in 1696 this became an independent church. Then in 1727 Blaenau Gwent combined with Llanwenarth and the Llanharan/Llantrisant Church (now moved to Hengoed) to found a Baptist church at Penygarn, Pontypool (i.e. Tabernacle). In 1747 all four churches combined to form 'Tydu' (i.e. Bethesda, Rogerstone). Bethesda was the first Baptist church in the lower Western Valleys.

The Western Valleys became industrialised mainly between 1780 and 1850. At first, iron-manufacturing industries were set up, mostly in the region of the heads of the valleys. Then the emphasis changed to coal production. Immigrants flooded in and populations increased dramatically (the population of Tredegar which was 1,132 in 1801 was 25,544 in 1851).

From about 1820 there was a vigorous growth of the Nonconformist cause in these new industrial areas and by 1850 the triumph of Nonconformity was complete (with Baptists numerically one of the strongest denominations). As new churches were formed they sent out offshoots. These in time, became independent, and the process was repeated.

Thus, at the lower end of the Western Valleys, offshoots from Bethesda were established in a number of places, including Risca, where Moriah (Welsh speaking) was founded in 1835 and Bethany (English-speaking) in 1855. In turn, members of these two churches were involved in the founding of Hope, in 1880. The lineage of Hope may thus be traced back to the early churches established by John Miles.

(b) The Founding of Hope

Development came relatively late to Crosskeys. In the year 1880, very little of Crosskeys, as we know it now, was in existence. The 6" Ordnance Survey map for 1886-89 gives the name *'Crosskeys'* to a few streets adjoining and somewhat to the north of the Crosskeys Hotel. Below the railway bridge Woodland Place had been built, but there were open spaces beyond Woodland Place on the road to Risca and across the valley to the small settlement of Newtown (then in *'North Risca'*). Beyond Newtown, in the direction of Wattsville (which did not then exist) was a small, closely packed settlement clustering around a public house and known as Full Moon (from the name of the public house).

In 1870 a small group of members from Bethany, Risca, held occasional open-air services at Full Moon and these developed into regular preaching services which were conducted by Rev. T. Reeves, then pastor of Bethany.

In 1878 prayer meetings began to be held regularly in the house of Henry Shipton, in Newtown. Henry Shipton was an invalid and was completely bedridden but was, nevertheless, an indefatigable worker. A nucleus of believers was formed and the evangelical work of Henry Shipton was soon being supported by that of others including John Oliver and Robert Britton.

A Sunday School was formed in 1879 with Robert Britton as the first Superintendent. Classes were held in a small room in a house at Woodland Place. Weeknight services were also held in this room and these were conducted by Rev. Thomas Thomas (now pastor of Bethany) and Rev. Thomas Lewis (pastor of Moriah). Rev. Thomas Lewis soon left the district but Rev. Thomas Thomas played a particularly important part in nurturing the young cause and guiding its growth.

It was decided to build a chapel and the foundation stone of 'Hope' was laid on March 4th, 1880 by Mr. E.H. Watts, Chairman of Watts, Ward & Co., the owners of Risca Colliery. A public service was held in the Wesleyan Chapel in the evening. The principal speaker was Dr. Thomas the (recently retired) Principal of Pontypool Baptist College. (The College moved to Cardiff in 1892).

The plans for the new building, which was to seat 800, were drawn up by Rev. Aeron Davies, Barry and the contract for building the chapel and vestry was let to Mr. Thomas Williams, Cwmdows, Newbridge. A large sum of money was advanced for a short term, free of interest, by local gentlemen and this enabled building operations to commence.

In July 1880 while the new church was in process of construction there was a serious explosion in Risca Colliery and many lives were lost including those of some of the most faithful supporters of the new cause. However, building continued and the vestry was soon complete. Such was the enthusiasm that although the vestry was still in use on weekdays as a workshop, it was immediately utilised for Sunday services. Each Saturday afternoon members cleared away tools, boards, shavings etc. so that Sunday services could be held.

A church was now formed. At first there were 33 members most of whom, although living in the Crosskeys area, had been worshipping in neighbouring Baptist chapels up or down the Valley. Four deacons were elected: Henry Shipton, John Tebbatt, Robert Britton and W.G. Edwards. These were installed in office by Rev. Thomas Thomas.

The first Sunday School Anniversary was held at Trinity, Pontywaun and the choir was provided by Bethany. A demonstration was held on the Monday when 70 children walked in procession and then were entertained to tea. The Sunday School Superintendent was Rev. Thomas Thomas; he was succeeded by Mr. W.G. Edwards (Headmaster of Waunfawr School).

A Sunday School treat organised later on in the year took the form of a trip by horse-drawn barge down the Monmouthshire Canal to the Cefn. The children were given tea in the vestry of Bethesda and then took part in sports which were organised in a nearby field.

In 1881, before the new chapel had been opened, the young church decided to give a call to Mr. (then Rev.) C.H. Watkins of Pontypool Baptist College. Mr. Watkins accepted the call and became Hope's first pastor.

Shortly after this a second explosion occurred at Risca Colliery. Few lives were lost but the decision was taken to close the colliery. This had serious consequences, for a number of workmen left the district and the young church, seriously weakened numerically, was soon struggling for funds. However, Monmouthshire Baptist Association furnished support and there were also generous contributions from members of Moriah and Bethany. This enabled Hope to continue to pay the small stipend of its new pastor.

Hope Chapel was finally completed and furnished and the opening services were held on February 18th, 1882 and on the three Sundays following. Preachers officiating at these services included Rev. W. Thomas of London, Rev. R. Lloyd of Castleton and Rev. T. Thomas of Bethany.

Bethany presented a communion service to Hope and also loaned a harmonium to lead the hymn singing until the new church was able to raise subscriptions to buy an instrument of its own.

It is worth noting that, prior to the erection of Hope Chapel, baptisms were carried out in the river Ebbw at Pandy bridge. It is recorded that *these ceremonies attracted great attention and were the means of making new converts'*.

Hope Baptist Church, Crosskeys.
Note Old Sunday School building at rear; see Appendix.

Hope Baptist Church, Crosskeys.
The Interior.

The First Two Ministries

Rev. C.H. Watkins (1881-1893)
Rev. W. Evans (1894-1914)

Most unfortunately, no full account can be given of the Ministry of Rev. C.W. Watkins. The relevant church books have been missing for very many years. But it is clear that Hope grew and flourished during this time. Rev. C.H. Watkins displayed remarkable organising ability and the future of the new church was soon assured. When, in 1893, Mr. Watkins accepted a call to Splott Road, Cardiff the membership of Hope had grown to *'between 200 and 300'.*

After Mr. Watkins' departure Hope was without a pastor for about 12 months. Then at a deacons' meeting (25.3.94) it was resolved to bring the name of Rev. William Evans, Llangynidr, before the church and this was done (1.4.94). An approach was to be made to Mr. Evans who was to be offered a salary of ten pounds a month plus *'a house and firing'* (the deacons were empowered to offer *'up to £12 - if necessary'*). Mr. Evans accepted the call and the conditions offered initially and his ministry commenced on August 12th, 1894.

Pastor's Vestry (built 1920).
Photographs of the first minister Rev. C.H. Watkins (1881-93)
and of Rev. A. Harries (1926-29).

There was as yet no manse and the Evans' lived in a house in Station Road rented from the G.W.R. The deacons had for some time discussed the possibility of building a new manse on a site which had yet to be selected. Policy was then changed. It was agreed that Westwood Villa should be purchased and a sum of £800 was paid for the property (4.11.94). This was quite a large sum to be expended by the new church which still had a considerable mortgage on the chapel buildings. It was covered by securing a loan of £700 at 5% interest from the Tydu Lodge of Oddfellows (17.12.94).

A major event in the life of the new church took place a short time before the actual commencement of Mr. Evans' ministry. This was when the Quarterly Meetings of the Monmouthshire Baptist Association were held at Hope for the first time. These meetings lasted two days and were held on Tuesday and Wednesday May 29th and 30th, 1894.

The morning of the first day was traditionally devoted to a general discussion of topical events. Excitement was heightened by the sudden, apparently unexpected, arrival of Mr. Lloyd George, M.P. who spoke about his attitude to the Welsh Disestablishment Bill (the proposal to disestablish the Anglican Church in Wales). It is recorded that Mr. Lloyd George was *'accorded a splendid reception and a hearty vote of thanks was passed'*.

Another interesting point is that during discussion on this first day the proposal was advanced that the time was now ripe for the formation of a Welsh Nationalist Party which would be independent of, but not necessarily hostile to the Liberal Party of the day.[4]

The Association preaching services commenced on Tuesday evening when services were held in Baptist churches in Newbridge, Abercarn, Risca and Rogerstone as well as at Hope. At each church two sermons were preached, one in English and one in Welsh.

On Wednesday all roads led to Hope. The day commenced with a service at 7 a.m. when Rev. J. Evans of Nebo, Ebbw Vale preached in Welsh and Rev. W. Thomas of St. Mellons in English. At 10 a.m. there was an open-air service with sermons by Rev. W. Griffiths, Rhymney (in Welsh) and Revs. W. Morgan, Pisgah and K. Lloyd, Castleton (in English). At 2 p.m. there was an afternoon service in the church (with two further sermons being delivered) and at 6 p.m. there was the evening service with a further three sermons (two in English and one in Welsh).

Thus, during the day, no fewer than ten sermons were delivered.

When Mr. Evans took office at Hope, membership of the diaconate was as follows: R. Britton (Treasurer), S. Bundy, J. Tebbatt, W.G. Edwards, D.W. James, J.G. Broakes, Wm. Jones, G.H. Nurse and Worthy Adams. The Church Secretary was J.E. Morgan.

At this time the membership of Hope was growing. It continued to grow under the ministrations of Mr. Evans. We read *'there are many candidates for baptism'* (23.3.97) and a little later that congregations were increasing so much that consideration had to be given to increasing the seating capacity by procuring light benches to be placed along the aisles when the chapel was full (27.9.02). Then, during the 1904-05 Revival there were plans to enlarge Hope (4.4.05) by rebuilding.

It is difficult to believe that despite the growth and health of Hope, these early years of Mr. Evans' ministry were sometimes attended with financial difficulties, since the coal industry at this time was in a depressed state. Time and time again the minutes record that *'collections do not yield enough to cover current expenses'* and there were frequent appeals and special collections. When the infant Baptist cause at Cwmcarn (established 1892) which had been using the local Board School's building for Sunday School and weeknight services, requested permission *'to raise funds to secure a more comfortable building'* the reply from the mother church was unaccommodating (4.8.95). *'There could be no thought of further commitments until Hope's own debts were reduced'.* Cwmcarn could collect - but only to help Hope.

With Lloyd George's recent visit in mind one of the deacons suggested (6.8.95) that *'the pastor should negotiate with the great man to try to get him to deliver a lecture at Hope. The proceeds from this could be used to reduce the debt on the chapel'.* Alas, nothing appears to have come from this ingenious proposal.

These early years, although successful, must have left their mark on Mr. Evans. Never robust, he now suffered constant ill health and at one point (when the worst of the financial crisis was over) he was obliged to take three months leave of absence from Hope. The death of his wife (16.12.95) must also have been a heavy blow.

It was in 1897 that the financial troubles appear to have started in earnest. Mr. Evans' salary should, by previous agreement, have been increased from £10 to £12 per month. Now in 1897 the increase was made - but it was already eight months overdue. Even so, with characteristic generosity, Mr. Evans offered to help the church by foregoing this salary increase for a further period. However, the church would not hear of such a thing (20.9.97).

It is possible that the church's financial embarrassment was compounded by the (to us) extremely unorthodox way in which money was being handled. We read a resolution (30.1.98) that *'all monies collected for the current expense account should be .... banked.'* It is difficult to realise that the idea of putting church money in the bank was, apparently, quite a controversial issue at this time.

Robert Britton, founder deacon of Hope, tireless worker and Treasurer for many years took exception to the above resolution which to him appeared to be an intrusion into his responsibilities as Treasurer. He maintained moreover, that banking was *'expensive and unworkable'*. Not only did he positively decline to bank the church monies in his possession but he also consistently refused to produce his books to the Secretary. This stand, made on principle, was nevertheless the stand of one man against the rest of the church. Inevitably, the motion was that *'the Treasurer be asked to resign his position'* and this was carried unanimously (30.1.99). Shortly afterwards the name of Robert Britton disappears from church records (it is known that in 1903 he was in membership in Bethany).

Financial difficulties were at their worst in 1899. The strain must by then have been beginning to tell for there are complaints that *'the financial conditions are due to the lack of spiritual life in the church and to the inactivity of the officers'* (5.6.99) and that *'the same members are contributing all of the time'*. Once more the cause at Cwmcarn appealed to be allowed to collect funds to improve its accommodation and once more the reply had to be that *'the time is not yet expedient'*. At this stage the new Treasurer, the veteran John Oliver, himself a Cwmcarn man, felt obliged to submit his resignation (it was subsequently withdrawn).(10.7.99)

In August 1899 drastic steps were necessary. Once more Rev. William Evans offered to take a reduction in salary (from £12 to £10 per month). Two years ago the church had regarded this as unthinkable. Now, they could only accept this generous offer with gratitude (20.9.99).

However, the worst was soon to be over. The church appears to have attacked its problems with increased vigour. At the same time conditions in the coal industry started to improve. In 1901 the current account was in

*Rev. William Evans
(1894-1914).*

credit for the first time for some years (14.1.01). By the end of the year the financial crisis was over and the Pastor's salary had been restored to its previous level.

It is of interest to look at Hope in 1903. Membership then stood at 350 and was increasing. There were between 400 and 500 children in the Sunday School (when these, together with the 200 children from the branch Sunday School at Cwmcarn, took part in the annual Sunday School Demonstration it must have been an impressive sight). The Sunday School Superintendents at Hope and Cwmcarn, respectively, were: Mr. C. Griffiths and Mr. T. Dight. A Band of Hope, conducted by Mr. T. Carter, met on Monday evenings and there was also a Ladies Sewing Class. On Thursday evenings the Young People's Bible Class met; this was led by the Pastor. In the summer months the morning service on Sundays at 11 a.m. was preceded by an open-air service at 9.30 a.m. which was taken by the deacons, in turn.

In 1896, John Collier, Hope's first candidate for the Baptist Ministry entered Cardiff College. (The Rev. John Collier was subsequently ordained and inducted as pastor of the historic Baptist church at Hay-on-Wye).

The minutes of a deacons' meeting held in 1898 are of interest. *'It is agreed that the Governors of Intermediate Schools should have use of the Schoolroom at Hope as an Intermediate Day School at a rent of ten pounds per annum'* (2.2.98). These minutes record the birth of Pontywaun County School (latterly Pontywaun Grammar School) now, alas, no more. The school subsequently moved to new buildings in Pontymister.

When the financial difficulties had passed, thought could be given to building much-needed Sunday School accommodation for the branch cause at Cwmcarn. It was resolved to make a start on this (9.9.02) but the actual commencement of building seems to have been delayed somewhat. The building at Cwmcarn was finally opened on April 23rd, 1913.

In 1905 it was agreed that a cause should be commenced at Wattsville (25.9.05). A Sunday School was started and classes were held in the home of Mr. David James, 15, Duffryn Terrace. This Sunday School soon had a membership of 120. Two classes occupied the front room of the house, one was held on the stairs and the other in the kitchen: Weeknight prayer meetings were also held in the same house.

14

The church at Hope agreed that a building site should be sought in Wattsville and that building operations should commence as soon as possible. (25.9.05). Volunteers were soon being called for to reduce expenses by assisting with cutting the foundations (13.8.06) and the church building, which was of corrugated iron construction was rapidly completed. Opening services were held on 23rd September, 1906 and on two Sundays following and the Rev. William Evans was given leave from his own Sunday School class to reorganise the Sunday School at Wattsville. A Band of Hope and Young People's Meetings were also started (13.1.08).

The new building was for a time leased to the local Education Committee for use on weekdays as a school for infants (11.11.06).

Although very much an offshoot of Hope the new church slowly started to gain its autonomy. Four deacons were appointed (4.11.10) and in 1910 there were discussions with Hope concerning the possible appointment of an assistant pastor (2.2.10). In 1909 Monmouthshire Baptist Association agreed that the Wattsville cause should be one of four small churches in Monmouthshire which would receive special attention and assistance (26.7.09).

An election of deacons was held at Hope in 1906 and the following were chosen: John Tebbatt, J.E. Morgan (Secretary), John Oliver, George Petheram; W. Watkins, Walter Westcott, Thomas Carter, A.E. Benson, Howell Pugh (Treasurer), D.R. Davies, John Coles and Edward Dight. (The Church Secretary had previously been J.G. Broakes and when J.E. Morgan resigned in 1908 A.E. Benson succeeded him).

When Hope was opened in 1882 subscriptions were raised to purchase 'a handsome harmonium to be used to accompany hymn singing'. This instrument was installed on the main gallery opposite the pulpit (the place is now occupied by a small, three-seat pew). In 1909 it was decided that the time had come to consider the installation of a new organ (8.10.09). A tender from the firm of J.J. Binns to deliver and install the pipe organ selected for £400 was accepted and the new organ appears to have been placed in its present position in 1912.

The original lease of the land on which Hope was built was granted by the London and South Wales Coal Co. but on 7.12.94 this was surrendered to one given by Lord Tredegar. Some years later it was discovered that the list of trustees was incomplete and 12 new trustees were elected in 1910. They were: John Tebbatt, J.E. Morgan, W. Westcott, G. Petheram, Thomas Carter, W.M. Watkins, A.E. Benson, E. Harries, W. Lovell, J. Cooper and J. Beale (16.10.10).

The year 1914 was momentous. At first, though, the outbreak of war with Germany made very little real impact on life in the Welsh valleys. Some young men were away in the army and navy but there was no conscription and the war must have seemed to be very far away.

So far as Hope was concerned the year 1914 was the milestone when the two branch churches at Cwmcarn and Wattsville became fully independent.

Zion, Cwmcarn achieved the new status first. A Hope Church meeting decided (2.4.14) that the cause at Cwmcarn should now be a separate church and a list of members of Hope who were to be transferred to Cwmcarn was drawn up (5.7.14). A few months were needed before the decision could be fully implemented because separation involved a certain amount of financial 'tidying-up'. There was still a debt of £1700 to be carried by the new church (the cost of erecting the chapel). This was far too great a load to be carried by a small, new church and after discussion, Hope agreed to accept half of this debt (29.5.14).

At this time, Rev. William Evans, now 63 years old, announced that he proposed to retire (9.8.14). The news must have come as a profound shock. Mr. Evans had been pastor of Hope for nearly 20 years and most of the congregation must have felt that any change was unthinkable. The news caused turmoil and was received by the church with profound regret and strong emotion.

Mr. Evans had served as pastor of Hope for a long time and the degree of pastoral care exercised by him was literally unique. He was one of the kindest, most understanding and saintliest of men. He was assured of Hope's confidence in him and undiminished love for him.

Mr. Evans preached from the pulpit of Hope, as Minister, for the last time on Sept. 6th, 1914. (In fact he was to occupy the same pulpit on many occasions during the next twenty years, especially when Hope was without a pastor).

At a public meeting held in Hope on 30.9.14. Mr. Evans was presented with a testimonial and 'a purse of gold'. The oldest member of Hope, Mrs. Henry Shipton, made the presentation. The meeting was well attended and no fewer than 18 Baptist ministers, mainly from local churches, were among those present.

The Years 1914-1918

Hope was without a pastor until Rev. Elwyn Williams was appointed in March, 1918. Vigorous attempts were made to replace William Evans and the church was balloted on a number of occasions (some of the ballot papers cane back with the name of Mr. Evans written in!) but no minister was appointed.

Immediately after Rev. William Evans' retirement, Bethel, Wattsville asked formally for its independence (9.10.14). This was granted (19.10.14) and a list was drawn up of those members of Hope who were to be transferred to the membership list of Bethel (1.11.14). Mr. Evans, who had been a moving spirit in the formation of Bethel in the first place, agreed to act as pastor of the new church for 'whatever stipend they could aftord' (9.10.14).

While at Wattsville, Rev. William Evans continued his association with Hope, often in an unofficial capacity. In 1916, when Hope was still without a minister the church recorded its thanks to Mr. Evans for continuing with his pastoral duties (most unostentatiously and without pay!). A small grant was made to cover his expenses (6.11.16).

As the years went by grim reminders started to come in of a world at war. On Sunday, October 10th, 1915 an appeal was read out from the Baptist Church at Hartlepool which had been destroyed by shellfire during a bombardment of, the north east coast by German battle cruisers. Names started to come in of boys from Hope who were injured or killed and the seriousness of the food situation became apparent as food prices skyrocketed.

Yet, in Hope, after the golden years of the ministry of William Evans and after the departure of so many members to Bethel and Zion, things must have seemed to go a little flat.

The manse was leased to the United National Colliery Co. for 14 years at £75 per annum. Discussions started (and these were to last a long time) about the purchase of individual communion glasses to replace the communion cups then in use. With the new organ occupying space which had been used by Sunday School classes there was now a shortage of accommodation and it was decided to build two small rooms at the side of Hope, along the boundary wall with the Co-operative Stores. Earlier on it had been suggested that this shortage should be solved by purchasing Nos. 2 and 4, Oak Terrace, for conversion to Sunday School use - but this was not followed up.

In 1915, Rev. E.H. Dight, a former member of Hope, was ordained at Oswestry.

Early in 1918 came the sad news of the death of Rev. William Evans' only son, Captain Jones Evans on the Western Front. The news came through early one Sunday morning and it is a measure of the inner strength of Rev. William Evans that, though frail in health and utterly heartbroken by his loss he walked, as was his way, from his home in Risca to preach the morning sermon at Bethel, Wattsville. (The name *'Captain Jones Evans'* is on the bronze memorial tablet now on the right hand side of the pulpit (25.10.20). This tablet also bears the names of: Bombardier Charles McGregor, M.M., and Privates Frank Dollery and Willie Lott.

The Years 1918-1925

(a) The Ministry of Rev. Elwyn Williams (1918-1923).

The recognition services of Rev. Elwyn Williams, Hope's third pastor, were held on July 6th, 1918. The pastorate lasted a relatively short time (until 2.12.23) but these post-war years were years of change and difficulty.

During the war, wages in the coal industry (as elsewhere) had risen dramatically but now, in the immediate post-war years the fall was just as dramatic. The coal industry was not in good shape and once again, as in the past in similar circumstances, Hope was experiencing financial trouble. At one stage, for instance, the Pastor's salary had to be reduced from £6 to £5 per week (2.5.22).

Moreover, and this was more important and was in sharp contrast with the pre-war years, there was now a widespread spiritual malaise in the churches. There are references in the minutes to the *'poor state of spiritual life at Hope'* and to poor attendances at weeknight meetings and to the *'leakage from the Sunday School'*. At one stage the deacons commenced a programme of visiting members in their homes in an attempt to improve matters (16.12.19).

Of course, the same sort of thing was happening in churches all around. But members of Hope with memories of the thriving church and large congregations of the pre-war era must have been sorely worried. It was a difficult time to be a pastor of a church.

In 1920 the two schoolrooms bordering the boundary wall with the Co-operative Society Stores were finally completed and then put to use by the Sunday School (24.3.20). During this year there were some changes at the front of Hope, when a portion of land was granted to the County Council so that road widening work could be carried out (16.1.20). Then in 1922 the freehold of Hope was purchased from the Tredegar Estate for £50 (31.5.22).

In 1919 some radical changes were proposed relating to the election and period of office of deacons and these were confirmed in a church meeting (20.10.19). It was agreed that the five most senior members of the diaconate i.e.W.M. Watkins, B.E. Harris, H. Pugh, H. Evans and H.T. Philipps should be *'permanent deacons'*, i.e. should serve for life, but that the remainder (T. Jones, T. Kenvyn, T.J. James, J. Morgan and A.E. Denning) should serve for only three years (but could then be re-elected). It was also proposed that four deaconesses should be elected; after discussion at the church meeting it was agreed to increase the number to six.

A ballot for deacons was held in 1920 (24.3.20) and an order of retiring agreed. Elected were G. Barnes, C. Winmill (Secretary), A.E. Denning, A. Williams, W.J. Williams, W. Drew, F. Hawkins, A. Callaghan, T. Carter and W.J. Lawrence (Treasurer). On the resignation of C. Winmill, W. Drew was appointed (19.11.20).

No deaconesses appear to have been appointed but this subject came up again in 1923 when the next triennial ballot for the diaconate was held. This time among the ten nominations received, was that of Mrs J. Binding (5.3.23). It is recorded that *'a long discussion took place regarding the position of a sister on the diaconate'* but it is clear that there was not felt to be any prima facie objection to the appointment of a woman deacon at this time. Indeed, there was a proposal to appoint all ten nominated persons since there were only ten vacancies (only two *'permanent deacons'* remained). However, Mrs. Binding declined to be elected *'without being voted on'*. After further discussion it was decided to elect only six deacons at that time (in fact seven were chosen because two polled equal numbers of votes). Elected were: G. Barnes, J. Binding, W.A. Drew, W.J. Lawrence, W.D. Osborne, W.H. Woodford and A. Williams (13.8.23).

The years 1922-23 were unfortunate in that relations between the pastor on one hand and the deacons and church on the other were sometimes less than happy. It appears that the decline in church membership was continuing. At one stage the entire diaconate resigned and a committee was appointed temporarily to carry out the functions of this body (2.11.22). Things had settled down again by early 1923 but Mr. Williams' pastorate came to an end on 2.12.23.

(b)   **1924-25**

After the departure of the Rev. Elwyn Williams, Hope was without a pastor for about two years. On occasion Rev. William Evans reappeared in the pulpit (he *'gave the charge'* to the newly-elected deacons on 2.3.24) but the church was largely dependent on *'supply'* preachers. One such was Rev. Arthur Harries of Splott Road, Cardiff. A strong impression was made on the church by Mr. Harries and, in 1926, he became Hope's fourth pastor.

In the years between pastorates there were several significant events. In 1925, for the first time in its existence Hope was debt-free. The mortgage on the chapel buildings had been paid off and the freehold secured. A Thanksgiving Service and Social Tea was held on 20.7.25. During the celebrations the Secretary, W.A. Drew *'gave the history of the church from the beginning to the end of Mr. Evans' pastorate in 1914'*. (It is unfortunate that no written record of this talk appears to have been kept!)

It is striking that at this meeting the theme coming through in the address of speaker after speaker is that Hope should not now *'rest on its laurels'* but should continue to raise funds, this time to erect a Sunday School building.

Thought had been given to this for some years and a Plans Committee met on 23.7.25 to discuss ways and means of implementing the idea. At first it was felt that the buildings of Salem, Blaina might serve as a model which could be followed by Hope but eventually it was decided to engage an architect to draw up new plans. Discussion of this project was, in fact, to extend over several years.

The Years 1926-33

(a)   The Ministry of Rev. Arthur Harries (1926-29)

The recognition services of Rev. Arthur Harries were held on February 24th, 1926 and the preachers were: Rev. T. Thomas (Bethany) in the afternoon and Rev. W. Evans in the evening. The three years of Mr. Harries' pastorate were most eventful years and the impact made on the church by the new pastor was powerful and long-lasting. Mr. Harries was a vigorous but erudite preacher, but, above all, an outstanding teacher. Hope was fortunate to have a man of such high calibre at the helm - even for a short time in these difficult years between the General Strike and the Depression.

Mr. Harries was soon outlining a scheme to make Hope more effective. Tracts were to be distributed within the district and special posters were to be displayed on the chapel notice board. Each candidate for baptism was to be given an advisory booklet and open-air services were again to be held during the summer.

New church organisations were also formed. A Bible School was started (5.7.26) with the pastor as principal teacher. A Sisterhood was commenced (23.5.27) the first officers being: President, Mrs. Harries; Vice President, Mrs. D. Osborne; Secretary, Mrs. T. Lewis; Treasurer, Mrs. Tregaskis and Organist, Mrs. O. Jenkins.

A Missionary Committee was also formed (2.5.27)

At a church meeting on 5.7.26 Mr. Harries urged that something be done to assist members of Hope who were in financial difficulties because of the current industrial crisis and it was agreed to take up a special retiring collection on two Sundays per month.

Under the previously-mentioned *'triennial rule'* some deacons were required to retire in 1926 and a ballot was held in which the following were elected: T. Carter, A. Williams, D. Osborne, M. Wilshire and J. Powell (3.5.26). At this time the election of deacons was again discussed by the church. There was a proposal that there should be annual elections. Mr. Harries disagreed pointing out that according to the Trust Deed, deacons should serve for life (*'once a deacon - always a deacon'*). Indeed, no further triennial ballots for the diaconate were held, neither did any member of the diaconate retire after three years. In the next ballots in 1934 three deacons were chosen and these were deemed to have been elected permanently (12.1.35).

From this time onwards the Trust Deed seems to have come into greater prominence in the life of the church. Earlier on it is seldom mentioned. Indeed, in 1922 (31.5.22) it was found that the original document had vanished and had been missing for some time. Over three years later the Committee which had been set up to look into the matter was still *'drawing up a new Trust Deed'* (8.2.26). But shortly after this, the Committee managed to locate the missing document which was displayed at a church meeting (19.12.26). Henceforth, this Trust Deed was sometimes to play an important part in determining church policy.

The Plans Committee (which was looking into the possibility of erecting a new Sunday School building) brought its ideas before the Church on 22.9.26 when it requested permission to get new plans drawn up by an architect. Plenary powers were given to enable the Committee to proceed with this. On 19.12.26 a new Committee was set up to find ways and means of raising money for the new project. However, somewhat later on there was consternation when it was learned that the cost of the building was likely to be in the region of £4000 (29.6.27). While the talks had been going on the financial state of the church had again been worsening (there was a bank overdraft of £35 on 26.10.27) and it was clear that the plans would have to be shelved for the time being.

However, there was further consternation when the architect's bill arrived - for £261.7.0 (13.2.26). Fortunately, following representations, this was reduced to £100.

In the minutes of the church meeting on 10.12.26 it is recorded that *'J. Pritchard and I. Powell have passed the lay preachers' exam'*. As Rev. John Pritchard and Rev. Ivor Powell these 'old boys' of Hope achieved eminence; the latter in his world-wide evangelical crusades and the former for his pastorates at Spurgeon's Tabernacle and at Leigh-on-Sea, as Minister of Mt. Albert Baptist Church, Auckland and finally as Principal of the Bible College at Henderson (near Auckland), New Zealand.

From July 2nd to October, 9th, 1927 Rev. A. Harries was away from Hope carrying out preaching engagements in the U.S.A. It is clear that his heart was very much in this type of work and on 2.1.29 he informed the deacons that he expected to receive a call to a church in the U.S.A. and that his resignation would take effect from 24.2.29. A delegation from the church pleaded with Mr. Harries to change his mind but he intimated that the decision must stand. A farewell tea for Rev. and Mrs. Harries was held on February 25th, 1929.

(b) **1929-33**

Following Mr. Harries's departure Hope was without a minister for nearly four years. During this time the Jubilee of Hope's founding was celebrated (in March, 1930). Jubilee celebrations lasted four days from Saturday, March 1st to Tuesday, March 4th (16.9.29).

On Saturday a meeting was held with Rev. Thomas Thomas (Bethany) in the Chair and Rev. William Evans giving the address. On Sunday there were services at 7 a.m. and 11 a.m. both taken by Rev. William Evans who also conducted the Jubilee Communion Service at 6 p.m. in the evening. On Monday there was a reunion of past and present members and on Tuesday afternoon there was a preaching service taken by Principal Chance of Cardiff Baptist College.

It was agreed that photographs of all past and present ministers should be obtained and hung in the church. A souvenir booklet was also produced, with a photograph of the founder, giving a brief history of the church (unfortunately no copies of this booklet appear to have survived).

These events were agreed to have been a splendid success (2.4.30).

On 25th May, 1931, Mr. Clifford Gay, a member of Hope, entered Dr. Howell's Bible School, London, to prepare for missionary service. Mr. Gay subsequently spent many years as a missionary in the Cape Verde Islands.

Discussions about the possibility of erecting Sunday School accommodation were again resumed (31.6.22). It was pointed out that there was a building, not now in use, at the Grwyne Fawr reservoir site (in the Black Mountains) which was relocatable and which could be erected at the rear of the church for use by the Sunday School. After further consideration it was agreed that this ingenious proposal was indeed feasible (24.10.32). The building would be far less expensive than one constructed more conventionally. The price being asked for the building was £120 and the total cost of the project was estimated to be in the region of £700.

In 1931, Monmouthshire County Council asked for a further portion of ground in front of Hope to permit the road to Carlton Terrace to be widened (9.11.31). The present walls and gates date from this time. Surplus stone from the old front walls (which were much higher) was stacked at the rear of the church and was then utilised in the Sunday School building.

Throughout these years the search for a pastor was continuing and on 16.1.33 it was decided to give a call to Rev. A. Glyn Davies of Pembroke.

The Years 1933-45

(a)   The Ministry of Rev. A. Glyn Davies 1933-42.

The induction services of Rev. A. Glyn Davies, Hope's fifth pastor, were held on 26th July, 1933 (with Rev. William Evans as Chairman).

Throughout 1933 work had been in progress on the Sunday School building. The corrugated iron structure from the Grwyne Fawr site was transported by a contractor to Crosskeys and then re-erected on a stone base at the rear of the church and the various stages of the operation were supervised by officers of the church. The total cost of erecting this building was £1036.

The Sunday School building was opened in November, 1933. It was an improvement which was long overdue. For instance, in 1933 there were 385 scholars and 30 teachers and officers on the Sunday School roll. Yet most classes were still being held in sometimes noisy surroundings in the open chapel. Now, with individual classrooms, conditions were greatly improved.

The Manse, Westwood Villa, had been leased to the United National Colliery Co. for 14 years in 1914 after the retirement of Rev. William Evans when Hope was without a minister. It was used as a Manse during the pastorate of Rev. Arthur Harries, but on his departure was rented by Mr. A.E. Benson, (Sunday School Superintendent, long-time deacon of Hope and former Church secretary). Now, in 1933, it became the Manse once more.

Up to 1934 Hope had been lit by gaslight but in that year electric lighting was installed (25.10.34). The cost of the installation was £21.5.0d.

The introduction of electricity enabled another improvement to be made. The pipe organ which had been installed in 1912 had a manually operated blower. On the right hand side of the organ, towards the rear, a long wooden handle projected. This handle had to be pumped up and down with some vigour when the organ was being played (the handle pumped a bellows which blew air into the organ pipes) and during the singing of hymns the congregation sometimes had a view, through chinks in a curtain, of a perspiring, shirt-sleeved brother hard at work. Now this could be changed. An electric blower was installed at a cost of £65 (25.10.34).

Elections for deacons were held in 1934 and again in 1939. In 1934 T. Kenvyn, E. Lane and B. Sainsbury were elected (12.11.34). In 1939 the new deacons were T. Morgan, A. Jandrell, I. Quilford and A.J. Carter (17.4.39). Other members of the diaconate in that year were: W.H. Woodford (Chairman), W.A. Drew (Secretary), D. Osborne (Treasurer and Asst. Secretary), H.T. Philipps, T. Kenvyn, B. Sainsbury, W. Williams and T. Lewis. In 1942 H. Dee, A. Denning, W. Jones and J. Powell became deacons (22.6.42).

The early years of Mr. Davies' pastorate saw growth in Hope. In 1934 the membership increased by 41 (there were 23 baptisms) and in 1935 the increase was 20 (14 baptisms). In 1935 the Bible Class was restarted and a Christian Endeavour was formed (13.11.35).

New Year's Party (circa 1935); Rev. A.G. Davies (1933-42)
in the foreground, to the right.

In 1936 the Government of the day introduced controversial Means Test Regulations. There were storms of protest in many parts of south Wales and in some areas churches combined to hold protest meetings. One such meeting was held locally and one of the aftermaths was the agreement to set up a United Church Committee. Such a committee would be able to deal with any emergency that might arise. It was obvious, too, that good could be done by united action in deepening the spiritual life of the area.

Hope sent three delegates to the United Churches Committee which was formed in the Crosskeys area (22.2.37) and for the next few years there was an improvement in liaison between local churches belonging to different denominations. Ministers exchanged pulpits, there were united services (e.g. on Good Friday 1937) and the annual Sunday Schools Demonstrations became one joint function.

Over the years 1937-40 the membership of Hope fell steadily (from 287 in 1937 to 222 in 1940) although this was largely due to movement out of the area. At the same time there was some concern about finances. For some months income had not been keeping pace with expenditiure and economies had to be made. The salary of the pastor had to be reduced from £5 per week to £20 per month and the caretaker's wage was cut from £1.5s.0d to £1.0s.0d per week.

World War II broke out in September 1939. As in World War I the initial effects on the Crosskeys locality were not great. Young men left to join the forces (but there was little active fighting at this time). Food was rationed and a 'black-out' imposed. Warning notes were occasionally heard from the siren mounted on Risca Urban District Council's offices and from the Risca Colliery hooter, but these were mainly practice runs.

Hostilities really commenced in Western Europe in 1940 and during the autumn and winter of that year the night skies above Crosskeys were often loud with the droning of German bombers on their way from bases in W. France to attack targets in the Midlands. Fortunately, few bombs fell in the immediate locality (although one evening two small incendiary bombs came down on the hillside just behind Hope).

Evacuee children had been moved into the area and for some time part of the Sunday School was used as day-school class rooms for children who had been evacuated from Poplar in E. London.

Hope carried on much as usual. Windows were curtained with heavy material and for a short period the time of Sunday evening services was changed to 5.30 p.m. (to utilise hours of daylight).

In 1942 Rev. Jack Gardiner was ordained as a Baptist Minister. Prior to entering Spurgeon's College, London, to train for the Ministry Mr. Gardiner had been very active in Hope as teacher of the Young Men's Sunday School Class and as Assistant Secretary of the Band of Hope.

In 1942 a Junior Christian Endeavour was started; the leaders were Mr. and Mrs. W.D. Osborne.

The year 1942 also marked the end of the pastorate of Rev. A.G. Davies. He submitted his resignation and this was accepted (22.6.42). Mr. Davies was a fine preacher and a good pastor. The early years of his pastorate had been particularly successful and he had baptised many converts.

(h)   The Years 1942-45

At home, these were years of strict austerity. Food and clothing were rationed and many items were unobtainable. Young men were mostly away in the Forces (including a number from Hope) and older men were enrolled as firewatchers, in the A.R.P. organisation or in the Home Guard. Some 'Bevin Boys' were drafted into the area to work in the coal mines. Seven days a week, convoys of buses moved down the Valley's roads, carrying shift workers to the war industries the aluminium works at Rogerstone and the explosives factories at Caerwent and Glascoed.

In the abnormal atmosphere of these wartime days there was little chance of expanding Hope's activities. There was also little chance of appointing a pastor. By the end of 1942 the loan raised to cover the cost of the Sunday School buildings had been repaid and Hope was again debt-free (12.12.42) but, at that time there could be little rejoicing.

The Church Secretary, W.A. Drew, moved out of the area and in 1943 he tendered his resignation. He was succeeded as Secretary by A.J. Jandrell (4.3.43).

In 1945 Hope gave a call to W.H. Davies of Cardiff Baptist College and he became Hope's sixth Pastor.

For some years the upkeep of the Manse, 'Westwood Villa' had posed problems. The decision was now taken to sell the property and a smaller house in Carlton Terrace was purchased. Mr. and Mrs. Davies were soon in residence in the new Manse.

The Pastorate of Rev. W.H. Davies - 1945-54

The year 1945 was most memorable. The wars in Europe and the Far East ended. Demobilisation soon started and the young men and women from Hope who had served in the Forces began to return home. But a small brass plate in the pulpit bears the names of four who did not return: George Bailey, Donald Kembrey, Melvin Clark and Reg. Jill.

This time there were no memorial plaques or Rolls of Honour to commemorate the war service of members of Hope. Instead, it was decided to install an improved lighting system in the chapel and to dedicate it to their memory. The new system was installed in 1947.

The atmosphere in Britain in 1945 was invigorating. There was still much austerity but with the end of the war new horizons had opened. In W.H. Davies, Hope had a new pastor to match the spirit of the times. The Church and its auxiliaries were soon thriving (membership of the Church stood at around 250 for much of Mr. Davies's pastorate). There was a strong and very active Young People's Fellowship. Great importance was attached to the Bible Class which had been restarted by the Pastor and the practice of holding Easter Conventions in association with the Bible Class soon became established. In 1947 A.J. Jandrell resigned as Church Secretary and W.D. Osborne was appointed to succeed him. In the same year K. Hibbs, a member of Hope who had served overseas with the Forces during the war, entered Cardiff Baptist College to train for the Ministry.

In 1946 came news of the death of Rev. William Evans. More than fifty years ago he had been inducted as Pastor of Hope and twenty years later had retired to take charge of Bethel, Wattsville (his last appearance

Rev. W.H. Davies (1945-1954).

in the pulpit was in 1937 - at the age of 86!). Now on 4.3.46 the grand old man was called to rest after a lifetime of the most exemplary service and sacrifice.

Rev. W.H. Davies left Hope in 1954 to become Minister of Tabernacle Baptist Church, Blackpool. He was a forthright, powerful and unambiguous preacher. Hope had flourished under his ministry and the influence of his pastorate was still being felt many years later.

1956-64

(a) **The Pastorate of Rev. Donald Gibbs B.D. - 1956-60**

Rev. Donald Gibbs, B.D. of Spurgeon's College became Hope's seventh pastor in 1956. The ministry of Mr. Gibbs, though relatively short, was vigorous and this was reflected in the continued level of activity in the church and its auxiliaries. Congregations, which had fallen somewhat in recent years, soon began to increase and church membership also increased.

An innovation introduced by Mr. and Mrs. Gibbs was the *'Sunshine Corner'* service for children on Sunday mornings. Mrs. Gibbs was the first leader of this children's meeting.

The last, small structural addition to the fabric of Hope was made in 1957. An extra room was created by roofing over the space between the kitchen and the end schoolroom. This was utilised as a Pastor's room.

Left to right - Tom Kenvyn, Islwyn Jones, Will Drew (former Secretary),
Donald and Mrs. Gibbs and family, W.D. Osborne (Secretary), W. Williams,
R. Goodfellow and Clarence Collins (circa 1958).

Bethel, Wattsville was without a pastor in 1956 and following a visit to Hope by a delegation of deacons from Bethel it was agreed that Mr. Gibbs should help Bethel by ministering to the sick and in weeknight activities (1.4.57).

In 1958 membership of the diaconate at Hope was as follows: A.E. Denning, R. Goodfellow, W. Williams, B. Hill, W.I. Jones, C. Collins, W.A. Drew (recently returned to the district) W.D. Osborne (Secretary) and T. Kenvyn (Treasurer).

In 1960 the Ontario and Quebec Convention conveyed to Mr. Gibbs an invitation to minister under the auspices of the Convention in E.Canada. Mr. Gibbs decided to accept the offer and submitted his resignation as Pastor of Hope. A farewell tea was held on Saturday, 23rd July (the last day of the pastorate) when presentations were made to Mr. and Mrs. Gibbs.

(b)   **1960-1964**

After Mr. Gibbs' departure Hope was without a pastor for four years. To be without a pastor for so long a period undoubtedly puts a great strain upon a church but it says much for the dedication, loyalty and ability of the officers and members of Hope that the chuch has been able to survive several intermissions of this length in recent times.

In 1962 the church organ, which had been showing signs of its age, was completely overhauled by the John Compton Organ Co. It was recommissioned at a service held on 23.9.62.

In the same year the Government indicated that it proposed to introduce new licensing laws for Wales. A delegation met the M.P. for Bedwellty, H. Finch, to put the views of the church on the matter.

1964-73

(a) The Pastorate of Rev. Lennard Jones, B.A. - 1964-67

In 1964, Rev. Lennard Jones became Hope's eighth pastor (6.6.64), the induction services being held on 2nd September.

Rev. Lennard Jones B.A. (1964-1967).

Membership of the diaconate had fallen to 6 and one of the first tasks facing the church was the appointment of new deacons. The following were appointed (23.6.65): G. Ashman, E. Jefferies, M.J. Parfitt and G. Walters. I. Jones became Assistant Treasurer (15.2.65) and G. Walters became Assistant Secretary (1.11.66).

In 1965 A.J. Jandrell who had been organist of Hope for 30 years indicated that he wished to resign. G. Hill was appointed as Mr. Jandrell's successor.

The freehold of the manse in Carlton Terrace was purchased in 1965 (5.4.65) and in that year the church was redecorated, the work being carried out entirely by the deacons.

At a deacons' meeting (12.10.65) the Pastor outlined plans for deepening the spiritual life of the church. He pointed out, in particular, the need for a Bible Class and for more prayer meetings (especially morning prayer meetings in homes or in the manse). Following discussion it was subsequently decided to form an Open Bible Class which would meet on Tuesdays (after Band of Hope) and also to form a Women's Fellowship to meet on Thursday mornings.

Progress was being made. However, on 16.6.67 Mr. Jones resigned and his pastorate ended three months later. He subsequently became Pastor of Hill Park Baptist Church, Haverfordwest.

(b)   **1968-73**

Over this period Hope was again without a pastor.

T. Kenvyn who had been associated with the church for many years, latterly as Treasurer, passed away in 1970 and the Assistant Treasurer, I. Jones succeeded him (1.5.70). The diaconate again became depleted and W.J. Jenkins and H. Jefferies were chosen to serve as deacons (15.11.72). In 1973, Rev. G.H. Duffett, a retired Baptist Minister from Winslow became Hope's ninth pastor.

1973-1982

(a)   **The Pastorate of Rev. C.H. Duffett - 1973-79**

Mr. Duffett's Induction Services were held on Wednesday, February 28th, 1973, the principal preachers being Rev. W.H. Davies (Blackpool) and Rev. I.J. Russell Jones (Moriah, Risca).

In 1973-74 there were significant changes in the diaconate at Hope. The Secretary W.D. Osborne now 80 years old, submitted his resignation (26.11.73) and was succeeded by the Treasurer, I Jones. Mrs. B. Jones became Treasurer. Early in 1974 Mrs. Duffett, Mrs. E. Hodge and Mrs. B. Jones joined the diaconate (26.1.74); these were the first deaconesses to be appointed at Hope.

Presentation to Mrs. Gladys Marsh (circa 1976).
Left to right - Ivy Parry, Gladys Marsh and Mrs. Duffet and Rev. C.H. Duffet.

In 1979 Mr. Duffett who was then 72 years old submitted his resignation and his pastorate ended in April 1979.

(b)   **1980-1982**

In 1982 it became necessary to appoint deacons once more. The following joined the diaconate: Mrs. P. Hill, Mrs. K. Jefferies, Mrs. V. Morgan, Mrs. M. Walters, Mr. J. Jefferies and Mr. D. Leyshon.

The centenary of the opening of Hope Chapel was celebrated in 1982. Services were held over the period Saturday March 13th to Sunday, March 21st. A notable feature of these services was the re-appearance in the pulpit of Hope of several former pastors.

An introductory tea was held on the opening Saturday; this was followed by an evening service at which the preacher was Rev. W.H. Davies (Blackpool). Mr. Davies also preached, morning and evening, on the following Sunday. On Tuesday there was a special service by the Band of Hope and on Wednesday evening a service with Rev. Lennard Jones (Barry) as preacher. On the final Sunday Rev. Donald Gibbs (Hayes, Middlesex) preached at morning and evening services.

1982

By mid 1982 Hope had been without a pastor for nearly four years. During intervals such as this, churches tend to decline, and the deacons felt the urgent need to appoint a pastor. Yet at this time Hope's financial position was such that it was not clear that a full-time appointment could be made, so a part-time pastorate was considered.

John Davies, a student at Cardiff Baptist College had preached at Hope on several occasions. He had apparently completed his studies, but because of ill health, had not taken up a full time ministry. John preached again at Hope (05.08.82) and again created a favourable impression, so much so, that the church decided to give him a call (23.08.82). It was originally proposed that he would exercise a part-time ministry; this later became full-time.

Rev. John Davies - 1982-1983

Ordination services were held at Nebo, Ebbw Vale, John's home church, on 13.10.82 and the Induction services were held at Hope on the following Saturday 16.10.82.

There was a problem with the Manse at 14, Carlton Terrace. It clearly needed repair and upgrading; in following years the church was to be involved in considerable expenditure here. Not until 1986 was it to be a pastor's residence again. But as a temporary measure, John lodged in the house of a church member.

This ministry appeared to start promisingly, with several baptisms, but this was not to last. The minute books report that *'an atmosphere of gloom was developing and attendance at services was declining'.* Moreover, the pastor appeared not to be in good health; on 25.05.83 doctors advised the deacons that the new pastor needed a period of rest. In fact, the ministry ended on 30.10.83.

This had been a very worrying time for all. But despite this apparent inauspicious start, Rev. John Davies has since conducted very successful ministries elsewhere in south Wales.

Towards the end of 1983 Hope was again without a pastor. But then an appointment was made in what might have been regarded by some as rather an unusual way.

David Leyshon was elected to the diaconate in 1982. At this time he was a policeman, stationed in Bettws but living in Pontywaun. But his background was hardly that of a typical police constable. David had attended Monmouth Grammar School; he then entered the University of Oxford (Lincoln College) where he obtained a First Class Honours degree in Modern History. He may have joined the police force as a University graduate, with the prospect of rapid promotion. But for some time things had been working in David's mind.

Rev. John D. Davies (1982-1983).

As a member of the diaconate he soon established a reputation for dedication and hard work and, more impressively, as a powerful preacher with a Bible-based message. Early in 1983 he felt God's call to the ministry and he had plans to enter Cardiff Baptist College to embark on the four-year course for the Diploma in Theology; this in the coming autumn. But for some months there had been doubts in his mind about this proposed move to Cardiff. To an able and committed Christian, already a University graduate, the prospect of another long academic *'apprenticeship'* must have been unalluring. David had already demonstrated his calling and his ability in the pulpit. There was a strong call to preach God's word - now!

After discussion with the deacons, already impressed by his talents and commitment, it was felt that David could serve now as *'Hope's spiritual leader and Under-Shepherd'*. This was confirmed at a church meeting (07.11.83). It was agreed that David would complete a correspondence course in theology, lasting four years, at Bryntirion Evangelical College.

In some quarters this might have been regarded as a bold experiment, for David had received no formal theological training. Things might have gone wrong - but they didn't! The deacons' judgement was justified and David Leyshon's pastorate, which lasted for fourteen years, until 1997, left its mark on the church. Having no theological qualifications he could not be styled 'the Reverend', in fact, the designation 'Pastor' fitted well.

The Pastorate of David Leyshon (1) - 1983-1986

Following David Leyshon's appointment (04.12.83), the atmosphere at Hope began to change perceptibly. Deacons' meetings, held rather sporadically not long ago, were now held monthly. A fortnightly Bible Study Group was formed. Family Services were introduced, as was a Summer Bible Class for children. A youth group was started and the library was upgraded. David's energy seemed boundless.

A vacancy on the diaconate was filled by Robert Anderton (11.01.84). There was another change in the diaconate when Pam Hill, a deacon since 1982, tendered her resignation.

At a deacons' meeting (26.09.84), some nine months after David's appointment, there was a stocktaking. Much had already been achieved. A different atmosphere existed in the church with increasing emphasis on evangelism. Eight baptisms had taken place and there was even a marked increase in the offerings.

Pastor David Leyshon and Deacons (circa 1985).
Back - Malcolm Parfitt, Mary Walters, Valwyn Morgan, Betty Jones (Treasurer)
and Islwyn Jones (Secretary).
Front - Kay Jefferies, Edna Hodge John Jefferies and David Leyshon.

In this new atmosphere though, controversial issues were sometimes raised. One of these concerned possible *'corporate membership'* at Hope; it was proposed that Hope should accept members from other denominations who had not been baptised by immersion - provided they were 'born again' Christians. But this was contrary to Baptist tradition; baptism by total immersion symbolising the New Testament doctrine of *'death, burial and resurrection'*. In time past the church's Trust Deed (a frankly Calvinist document, dating back to 1885) had been quoted in defence of this position. As had happened on previous occasions, once a division of opinion was revealed within the church, it was agreed to let the matter drop.

Another somewhat controversial measure, discussed briefly in these early days (but more fully later on), was the possible change in government of Hope by introducing elected elders. These would exercise spiritual leadership; the deacons would be more concerned with practical matters. A decision here was finally made in 1994.

A small but notable change in 1985 was the removal of the big deacons' seat at the front of the church. The author remembers the time when this seat, the sole preserve of the deacons, would have been fully occupied. Seen from the gallery there would have been a splendid profusion of white and hoary heads. But woe betide the one who inferred that hoary heads were a sign of decrepitude; he soon discovered that the white hair was an adornment and that there were very active minds beneath!

The limited space between the *'big seat'* and the baptistery rail had been something of a nuisance for years, especially during funeral services. Now in 1985, the seat was taken out.

Contact with former ministers of Hope was maintained over the years. Rev. W.H. Davies, Rev. Lennard Jones and Rev. Donald Gibbs all preached at the Centenary services held in 1982. Rev. W.H. Davies preached again at the Church Anniversary Service in 1985, Rev. Lennard Jones took these services in 1986; in 1984 Rev. Lennard Jones had been pastor of Bethel Baptist Church, Barry, for 25 years. Rev. Donald Gibbs returned to Hope on several occasions, once to conduct a healing mission.

Rev. Michael Thomas, who had attended Hope as a boy and had become Headmaster of Thomas Hardy's School in Dorchester before entering the ministry, was ordained at East Sheen Baptist Church, London, on 01.06.85. Michael's mother had been a very active member of Hope for many years.

The chapel was used for collaborative services with local churches. In 1984 and for some years afterwards a joint Remembrance Day Service was held with Trinity Congregational Church. The Crosskeys and District United Choral Festival was held regularly in November and on occasion, broadcast *'Songs of Praise'* services were held. During David's pastorate, a much closer relationship continued with Crosskeys Pentecostal Church and joint prayer meetings and open-air services were held. David preached in a number of churches in the district; a favourite venue was the Evangelical

David Leyshon and Deacons (circa 1997).
Back - Lyn Bevan, Stuart Godfrey, Robert Anderton (Secretary), David
Leyshon, Graham Roberts and Tony Biggs.
Front - Kay Jefferies, Debbie Leyshon, Betty Jones (Treasurer), Valwyn Morgan
and John Jefferies.

Church at Nant Coch, Newport. David would preach a sermon at Hope; then he would be whisked down to Nant Coch!

Waunfawr School held their annual Harvest Festival at Hope for a number of years and the church was also used by Cwmcarn School for the annual Christmas Carol Service. The Schoolroom was used as a polling station at election times up until 1994.

In 1986, as a form of outreach activity, a luncheon club was started designed for the elderly where an inexpensive meal was served followed by a Christian address. This venture was soon an obvious success. Also at this time a new magazine *'Good News for Crosskeys'* was developed jointly with Crosskeys Pentecostal Church. Later on, Hope published its own magazine *'Hope for the Future'*.

In 1986 the Manse became habitable and David and his wife Debbie moved in (12.09.86). At the Annual General Meeting in that year there was a feeling that after three years of David's ministry *'Hope had reached a turning point'*. During that year there had been eight baptisms and church membership (85 at the end of 1984) was now 95 and David had started a discipleship course for new members. But it was pointed out that that one area where improvement could occur was in the church's financial support of missionaries. In 1986 this accounted for 3% of income. A target of 10% was set for future years though later on this was to rise to 17% and then 25%! An ad hoc committee was set up to oversee this missionary support. Later on this became a missionary committee with Lyn Bevan as Chairman (25.09.92)

Pastorate of David Leyshon (2): 1987-1991

At the Annual General Meeting held in 1987 it was reported that Maria Spencer, a member of Hope, had felt a call to missionary service abroad. It was agreed to provide financial support for three years; one year at Bryntirion College to be followed by two years of language training in France. Maria's original intention was to work on the Ivory Coast, in West Africa, though subsequently, plans were altered.

A small change in the form of Sunday Services took place in 1988. It was agreed that before the opening of the Sunday evening service, Tony Biggs would lead a short period of prayer, readings and choruses, accompanied by Robert Anderton on the piano. In 1988 it was agreed, too, that Family Services would be held every Sunday morning, these had previously been restricted to the first Sunday of the month.

There was a proposal to form a new mid-week meeting in lieu of the Sisterhood and Men's Fellowship meeting. But both these meetings were already successful so the idea was dropped.

In 1989 a proposition of major concern began to be discussed. At this time ecumenical policies were attracting attention in most denominations. Following a meeting at Swanwick in 1987, the Baptist Union of Great Britain published an important policy document (the so-called 'Swanwick Declaration') which suggested the formation of much closer relationships with other denominations; David prepared a brief summary for use at Hope. An objection to the approach apparently being suggested in the Swanwick Declaration was that fundamental Baptist principles were being jeopardised. Moreover, in this 'ecumenical' approach, Evangelicals and Pentecostals appeared to have been excluded. This matter was to be discussed at intervals over the next two years before decisive action was taken.

On 29.03.89 a farewell tea was held for Mr. and Mrs. Thomas who were leaving the district to join their son, Rev. Michael Thomas, now pastor at East Sheen Baptist Church, nr. London.

David had expressed concern on a number of occasions about what he saw as the difficulty of obtaining a truly Christian education in the present system. Following discussion it was decided to start a new Christian School to be called Emmanuel School, in the old Sunday school classrooms at the rear of Hope Church. It was hoped that subsequently a more satisfactory building would be found. But this arrangement, envisaged as a temporary expedient, was to last for over twelve years. The school opened in 1990 with five pupils; although the buildings of Hope were used, this was, nevertheless, an independent school.

A group of members had been keeping an eye on the care and maintenance needs of the church and the Manse and a Fabric Committee (26.06.90) was set up to oversee this work. John Davies was the first chairman of this committee. John did a tremendous amount of work for the church, drawing up plans and working on projects. The interior of the church was completely redecorated under the auspices of the Youth Opportunity Scheme superintended by John Davies. On John's retirement (12.11.93) Graham Roberts became chairman.

The matter of ecumenism and the Swanwick Declaration came up again in 1990 (30.11.90). The position was now quite complicated. The Baptist Union of Great Britain voted to approve the development of the *'interchurch process'*. But the Baptist Union of Wales was split right down the middle. The Welsh-speaking churches approved the former decision. But the English-speaking churches opposed it. However, it had been decided (surely rather strangely!) by the Baptist Union of Wales, that if any one wing of the movement gave its approval, the other wing would be obliged to follow suit. Because of this some 6% of the English-speaking churches decided to break away from the Union and to become Independent Baptist churches. In what was a historic decision, Hope decided to follow this example and to withdraw from the Baptist Union of Wales (30.10.90).

Following this move, attempts were made to recover the church's Trust Deeds from the Baptist Union of Wales; this is quite a saga!

Pastorate of David Leyshon (3) - 1991-1997

When the question of the appointment of elders came up previously (11.11.91) it was agreed to defer discussion for two years. Discussions were held again at the end of 1993. David was strongly for the appointment of elders, citing New Testament precedents. But such a move appeared to be a considerable departure from what was regarded as well-established practice at Hope.

In fact, 14 elders were elected at Hope in 1894 (25.11.1894)! But in this case their functions would have been different; they were clearly subordinate to the deacons. David wished to elect two elders who were to exercise spiritual oversight; the deacons would then be concerned with practical matters.

Following a church meeting two nominations were received and a ballot was held at a special church meeting (10.05.94). To be elected an elder needed the support of two thirds of church members attending the meeting. In fact, neither candidate received this endorsement; one narrowly failing to do so. The idea was dropped.

One of the saddest pieces of news in the entire history of the church came to light at a deacons' meeting in 1992 (02.06.92). The pastor, David Leyshon, then 37 years old, revealed that he had been diagnosed as suffering from Parkinson's Disease. This was affecting his co-ordination and his mobility; moreover, he now became fatigued very rapidly. It was obvious that sooner or later, he would be unable to lead effectively, and five years later, in 1997 (03.08.97) he was obliged to tender his resignation.

The pathetic evidence of the progress of this terrible disease can be seen on the church Minute Books. The signature of David as chairman, once a bold flourish, had declined by 1997 to a pathetic little squiggle. This was a very cruel stroke. But David struggled on. Even in 1997 he had plans to deliver a leadership course for members of Hope working as auxiliaries.

In 1992 David was in touch with Fisseha Bekele, a pastor in Ethiopia; he had been a pen friend of David's for some years. Fisseha, a member of a branch of the Ethiopian Lutheran Church, had been active as a pastor and had established several small churches, this on a very low wage (£30 per month!). Following discussions with the church and a visit by David to Ethiopia, it was decided that Fisseha should be brought to this country for two years to train at Bryntirion Evangelical College near Bridgend. Hope decided to provide financial assistance for Fisseha and his wife Membre; they arrived in this country in August 1993.

Emmanuel Christian School continued to grow slowly Alison Scott, a qualified teacher from Alice Springs in Australia, joined the church in 1992 and in 1995 she took over the headship; at this stage there were 16 pupils, 2 paid full-time teachers, 4 unpaid full-time teachers and 2 unpaid part-time teachers.

From the first, it was realised that the premises at Hope, though a good temporary expedient were in some ways, unsuitable. Vigorous attempts were made to find alternative premises. At one stage it was proposed to amalgamate with a Christian School attached to a Baptist Church in Abersychan to use joint premises at Pontypool. But no long-term solution appeared and the school continued to use the old Sunday School classrooms at Hope. A further complication arose when it was discovered that fire regulations precluded the use of the upstairs classrooms so a move downstairs had to be made. Later the school shared with the church the cost of completely renovating the upstairs classrooms.

The Trust Deeds of the church were still being held by the Baptist Union of Wales. However, it was decided to form a board of trustees in preparation for a possible return of the deeds to Hope. The following were chosen: Islwyn Jones, Betty Jones, John Jefferies, Robert Anderton and Malcolm Parfitt; these were all deacons. The following church members also became trustees: John Davies and Graham Roberts (21.11.93).

Towards the end of 1995 there were vacancies on the diaconate; Islwyn Jones and Malcolm Parfitt had passed away.

Islwyn Jones had been associated with Hope for many years; he had been a deacon since 1958. Superintendent of the Band of Hope, Church Treasurer and Church Secretary since 1974, he had followed W.D. Osborne in these roles.

Malcolm Parfitt, a deacon since 1965 and Sunday School Officer was for some years a County Councillor. He was a patient and tireless worker, particularly effective as a chairman of meetings. On a number of occasions he had the unenviable task of taking the Chair of Deacons' and Church Meetings when controversial and potentially divisive issues were under discussion.

Hope Church was to miss these stalwart workers. As a memorial to both, the Church's sound system was improved.

New deacons elected on 16.01.96 were Tony Biggs, Stuart Godfrey, Graham Roberts and Lyn Bevan. Robert Anderton became the new Church Secretary and Stuart Godfrey the new Assistant Secretary (27.03.96). Tony Biggs was appointed Assistant Treasurer on 16.01.96. Edna Hodge, a deacon since 1974, now tendered her resignation as a deacon; Mary Walters a deacon since 1982 had resigned a little earlier on 12.10.94.

Fisseha, from Ethiopia, completed his studies at Bryntirion. At this time David Wilcox who with his wife Pauline had joined Hope from Moriah Baptist Church, Risca, felt that God had called him to work in the mission field; he sought to work in Albania under the auspices of the Albanian Evangelical Mission and was accepted. But in view of the unsettled state of

David and Debbie Leyshon and family with Hope Congregation 1997.

the country at that time they went first to Skopje in Macedonia. Hope provided financial backing.

For many years the Sunday School at Hope had met on Sunday afternoons; in many churches Sunday Schools met on Sunday mornings. Now a similar change was proposed for Hope. But sadly, over the years there had been a massive decline in the number of children attending; in 1997 there were just 30, though there were still 35 adults in adult classes. In a few years Sunday School and Band of Hope were to disappear completely.

David Leyshon struggled on at Hope for some years after the onset of Parkinson's Disease had been discovered. In 1997 (31.08.97) he announced his retirement. His pastorate, lasting 14 years was one of the longest in the Church's history, exceeded only by that of the Rev. William Evans (1894-1914). But William Evans ministered at a time when, under the influence of the 1904 Revival, churches were expanding rapidly; in David Leyshon's time the reverse was the case. His achievements were, in a sense, greater for this. His influence on Hope had been enormous and he was to be sorely missed.

A farewell Tea and Testimonial Meeting was held for David and Debbie Leyshon on 26.07.97. This meeting, quite literally, marked the end of an era.

1997-2001

After David Leyshon's departure, Hope was without a minister for nearly four years; it was not until 2001 that the Rev. Stephen Jackson was called to become the church's next pastor. In the interregnum a number of preachers occupied the pulpit at Hope and several were considered as successors to David. It was felt that since Hope had left the Baptist Union, Baptist ministers and students from the Baptist Colleges would not appear in the pulpit. Indeed, at a church meeting (24.02.98) a motion was proposed that Hope should rejoin the Baptist Union, but this was defeated. However, later on, Rev. Peter Manson, Baptist Area Superintendent for south Wales met with the diaconate to offer help in filling the pastoral vacancy (11.01.99).

At the Annual General Meeting of 1998 (23.09.98) it was agreed to revert to the old procedure whereby representatives of the auxiliaries appeared at the meeting to present reports. Membership of the Church was now 93. It was agreed to continue to devote 25% of the church's income to missionary work.

Stuart Godfrey, the Assistant Secretary resigned (14.09.98). Geoff Marshall (Bridgend) conducted a number of out-door services. A loop system for hearing aid users was installed in the church; the sound system was also improved by use of radio microphones (12.01.98). Graham and Mary Roberts resigned as editors of the church magazine 'Hope for the Future' (22.06.98); they had been editors for nine years.

Standing John Jefferies, Graham Roberts, Stephen Jackson, John Davies (Secretary), Stuart Godfrey and Bill Kelso.
Seated Kay Jefferies, Kath Jackson and Pam Kelso.

In 1998 the Church Secretary, Robert Anderton indicated that a revised version of the Church Covenant and Rule Book was in preparation; the present Covenant was drawn up in 1921 (04.02.21). Changes were suggested, all based on the original Trust Deed of 1885. The proposed revisions were agreed to unanimously at a Church Meeting (26.01.99).

Tony Biggs the Assistant Treasurer, who was moving out of the area, retired from the diaconate (21.06.99); he was replaced by Graham Roberts. Mrs. Betty Jones, Treasurer since 1974 (26.01.74) passed away this year and tributes were paid (13.07.99). Betty joined Hope in 1945 and became a deacon in 1974. It was subsequently decided to place a memorial plaque for Betty and her husband Islwyn (Church Secretary for many years) in the vestry.

(There is a gap in the minutes from July 1999 to December 2000).

At a Deacons' Meeting on 06.02.01 it was agreed that members of the diaconate would constitute the Mission Committee.

At this time, it was felt by all church members that there was an urgent need to appoint a new pastor. Hope had been without a pastor for nearly

3¹/₂ years following the departure of David Leyshon. As a preliminary step to a possible appointment, Rev. Stephen Jackson of Newbridge was invited to lead a Bible Study at Hope (22.01.01). He then met the deacons, was invited to serve as pastor and indicated his acceptance (25.05.01). His ministry commenced on 12.08.01. An Induction Service was held on 08.09.01 at 3.30pm. Rev. Stephen Jackson, originally a member of Beulah Baptist Church, Newbridge, studied at the Barry Bible College and the South Wales Baptist College, Cardiff. He had previously conducted ministries in Norwich and in Newbridge.

A very sad event occurring at this time was the death of Garrod Hill, the organist at Hope (14.03.01). Garrod had served as organist for many years; he followed A. Jandrell in this post in 1965. He had also served the church in other capacities including that of caretaker and general handyman. It was agreed to erect a memorial plaque to Garrod, in the church, in recognition of his many years service (15.10.01).

Mary Roberts became Church Organist (14.03.01).

Robert Anderton, Church Secretary for the last five years (from 26.01.96), indicated his intention to resign (17.07.01). Lyn Bevan agreed to act as Secretary temporarily. This was confirmed (26.06.01). John Woodford became Assistant Secretary. John Davies and Graham Rhodes were appointed to the diaconate (22.01.02).

It was agreed to hold open-air meetings with Crosskeys Pentecostal Church (25.03.02). It was also decided to hold a family service at Hope on the 3rd Sunday of each month. A sub-committee was set up to compile and oversee a Register of Church Members and to be involved in pastoral contacts; this committee comprised; L. Bevan, J. Davies, G. Rhodes and J. Woodford (22.04.02). It was agreed to hold meetings of the diaconate to deal with the church constitution.

2001-2005

At the Annual Meeting for 2002, it was noted that Rev. Stephen Jackson had now been pastor at Hope for some seven months. Changes were already apparent. The pastor pointed out that there was good reason to be thankful for the testimony of Hope Church, for its history, work, activities and warm friendship. Such qualities should be maintained. Looking to the future, there was a great need for evangelical outreach and to think of new ways of serving God as we seek to move in His purpose.

At this meeting John Davies was appointed Assistant Secretary and John Woodford became Minute Secretary. There were now 61 Members.

A Special Church Meeting was held (21.01.03) to discuss revision of and updating the Church Covenant. The New Rule Book was subsequently accepted at the Annual Meeting for 2003 (18.03.03). Church Membership was now 50, with a *'dormant'* list of 9.

It was pointed out (24.02.03) that the church conforms to the recent legislation on the protection of children. A list of regulations applying to people working with children has been placed on record. Megan Jones has had her membership transferred from Zion, Cwmcarn, to Hope. It was agreed that open-air meetings should be held again this summer, in conjunction with Crosskeys Pentecostal Church.

On Sunday April 25th Maria Hartiel (nee Spencer) and her husband Emmanuel spoke about their work in France; in particular about their plans for evangelical work in Belle Île en Terre.

It was agreed (02.06.03) that a Church Family Meal would be held on 23.07.03. Steps were being taken to form an organisation within the church for children within the 5-12 age group; at the first meeting (02.05.03) some 31 children attended. Known as the 'Ks', this was a clear success story. Meetings were held on Friday evenings.

The resignation was received, with great regret, of Valwyn Morgan (01.09.03); Valwyn had served as a deacon at Hope since 1982. Great appreciation was shown for her years of service; she was subsequently made an Honorary Life Deacon (23.09.03) and a presentation was made to her (07.10.03). There was now a need to elect more deacons. Nominations were called for and Pat Kelso, Bill Kelso, and Stuart Godfrey were proposed. All three candidates were subsequently elected (07.10.03).

Waunfawr School held their Harvest Service at Hope on 24.10.03.

Graham Rhodes, long-standing member of Hope and deacon since 22.01.02 passed away. It was agreed to purchase 80 bibles for church use; this in memory of Graham. A service of dedication and remembrance was held on Sunday 25th January 2004.

On 01.12.03 the resignation was received with regret of two church members Mel and Margaret Evans who were moving from the area. A presentation was made to them (14.01.04).

It was agreed (14.01.04) that Mary Walters should undertake the duties of the office of Community and Social Awareness.

The Christian Emmanuel School moved back to its original location, upstairs in the schoolroom; the school moved out of the church buildings by the end of 2003.

The resignation was received of the Church Secretary Lyn Bevan (02.02.04). Lyn and his wife Anne (who was also leaving Hope) were both to become members of the Baptist Church at Cefn Wood. Nominations for a replacement were called for; all of these were for John Davies, the Assistant Secretary. John was elected (08.03.04).

It was agreed not to appoint an Assistant Secretary at this time.

An Easter Mission was conducted at Hope by Rev. Glyn Morgan, from 4th-11th April 2004; a pre-mission rally was held on 28.02.04. This was a great success and the results were reviewed (19.04.04).

A welcome development in 2004 was the production of a printed report detailing the activities of the church during the previous year. This report was presented to the Annual General Meeting (30.3.04). In this report it was pointed out that during the year it had become necessary to implement some of the newer legislation involving Child Protection and Disability Discrimination. New safety issues have also had to be addressed; emergency lighting systems had been fitted in the vestry and back vestry.

Throughout 2003-2004 the activities of the Luncheon Club, the Sisterhood and the Mens' Fellowship continued, joined now by the new children's group the 'Ks'.

It was with great regret that the resignation of Stephen Jeffries, Secretary of the Mens' Fellowship, was received.

At the Annual General Meeting thanks were expressed to Lyn and Anne Bevan for their years of service to Hope. The revised Church Rules were adopted. The church was to join the Evangelical Alliance. Stephen Jefferies was to become permanent Auditor with Christine Clark as assistant.

The pastor had attended meetings of Gwent Baptist Association, necessarily as an observer (since Hope is not now a member of the association). However, he was asked to give a report on the recent Mission at Hope (12.05.04).

It was decided to make a change in the Tuesday Prayer/Bible Class Meetings. Once during each month a speaker from a missionary cause would be invited.

Westwood Villa, Crosskeys.
For many years this was the residence of Ministers of Hope Church.
(Taken with permission of the owner.)

Anne Bushell who had been acting as Church Function Co-ordinator did not wish to continue in that role; a team comprising Janet Davies, Ninette Rhodes and Pam Hall now took over this responsibility.

A Baptismal Class with three young candidates was started (28/09/04).

A decision was taken to join I.C.E. (Wales) [Initiatives in Christian Education].

Councillor Michael Gray very kindly sent the church a donation of £178; with other councillors he had agreed to forgo an increase in allowances, donating the money, instead to good causes.

At this time (28.09.04) the church was saddened to hear of the passing away of Rev. W.H. Davies; minister of Hope from 1946-52, before moving to Blackpool. Rev. W.H. Davies was minister of Tabernacle Baptist Church, Blackpool, for 44 years. He acquired a very considerable reputation as a preacher in the North of England; Rev. Martin Lloyd Jones once described him as *'The Puritan of the North'*! A letter of condolence was sent to Mrs. Vera Davies.

John Woodford, long time member of Hope and deacon announced his resignation (11.10.04). John was now to attend the Pentecostal fellowship in Newbridge where his wife had been a member for many years. Gail and Stephen Jefferies decided to transfer their membership to a cause at Brynithel; Bill Kelso was to replace Stephen as Church Auditor (06.12.04). A letter of best wishes was forwarded on to Gwyneth Parker who had moved to Cornwall.

Publicity material had been produced for five Sundays over the Christmas period, 2004, with details of the week of prayers on the back. On the 19th December the morning service was to involve communion and a special prayer and time for children; in the evening there was to be a Carol Service.

A letter was received from Don Touhig M.P. (07.02.05) concerning the Incitement to Religious Hatred legislation currently being discussed in Parliament, Don Touhig suggests that fears which had arisen over this legislation were unfounded. But concerns over the possible effects of this legislation had led to an important meeting in London, organised by the Christian Institute, to discuss matters more fully.

Mrs Bernice Pugh, a member of Hope for many years passed away as did Muriel Wheeler and her husband Clarence, Muriel and Clarence were active in Hope for many years, for a number of years acting as caretakers. The church recorded its thanks for gifts of £200 in memory of Muriel and Clarence.

The Annual General Meeting was held on 05.04.05. The Church Auditor Stephen Jefferies had moved to another fellowship and Christine Clark (Assistant Auditor) and Bill Kelso (Stephen's successor) were in the process of completing the audit so audited accounts were not immediately available at the meeting. The practice commended last year of producing a printed

Annual Report was continued this year. Reports covered the Sisterhood (Jayne Whitehouse), Men's Fellowship, the *'Ks'* (Childrens' Meeting), Luncheon Club, Mission Support Group, and Sunday School. It was pointed out that Hope has been strongly advised by the Health and Safety Executive and the Ecclesiastical Insurers to appoint a Safety Officer.

At the A.G.M. members read the Covenant and Statement of Faith aloud together, and re-affirmed their commitment to Baptist principles.

An important event, which took place on May 24th, was a visit organised by the Christian Institute. This was a great success (06.06.05).

Brian Collins a local author completed a book *'Crumlin to Pontymister; Places of Worship, A Sketchbook History'*. Several pages are devoted to Hope and photographs have been incorporated. It was published in November 2005.

Following Health and Safety Regulations, warning signs have been erected at several points in the church (14.11.05).

A full programme for missionary evenings on Tuesdays was finalised (04.10.05).

A Harvest Service was held at Hope on Sunday October 9th.

Waunfawr School held their Harvest Service at Hope on October 21st.

The year 2007 will mark the 125th Anniversary of the founding of Hope and a Committee was set up to organise events to commemorate this; the first meeting was held on 05.01.06. It was proposed that: - Anniversary Services conducted by Rev. Colin Lewis should be held on Sunday March 11th 2007, and that services should also be conducted by Rev. P. Manson, former Superintendant of the south Wales Area (Baptist Union) on Saturday 9th - Sunday 10th June 2007.

Other events proposed include performances by the Mynyddislwyn Male Choir and a Cymanfa Ganu with Crosskeys Choral Society.

Further developments can be anticipated.

APPENDIX

PART 1

List of Ministers of Hope Baptist Church

Rev. C. H. Watkins	1881-1893
Rev. W. Evans	1894-1914
Rev. Elwyn Williams	1918-1923
Rev. Arthur Harries	1926-1929
Rev. A. Glyn Davies	1933-1942
Rev. Donald Gibbs, BD	1956-1960
Rev. Lennard Jones, BA	1964-1967
Rev. G. H. Duffett	1973-1979
Rev. John Davies	1982-1983
David Leyshon, BA	1983-1997
Rev. Stephen Jackson	2001-
*Rev. W. H. Davies	**1945 – 1954**

PART 2

Members of Hope Church who have entered the Ministry and/or have carried out Missionary Work Abroad

1896   John Collier
John Collier, Hope's first candidate for the Ministry, entered South Wales Baptist College. He was subsequently ordained and inducted as Pastor of the historic Baptist Church at Hay-on-Wye.

1915   Rev. E.H. Dight
Rev. E.H. Dight, a former member of Hope, was ordained at Oswestry.

1928 John Pritchard and Ivor Powell
John Pritchard and Ivor Powell passed the Lay Preachers' Exam.

Rev. John Pritchard became a minister at Spurgeon's Tabernacle Church, London, then at Leigh on Sea, before becoming Minister of Mount Albert Baptist Church, Auckland, N.Z, then Principal of the Bible College at Henderson (nr. Auckland) N.Z.

Rev. Ivor Powell became known internationally for his world-wide evangelical campaigns, which took him to places such as N.Z., Australia and South Africa; he also preached extensively in the U.S.A. He lived in Santa Barbara, California, was the author of a number of books and was awarded a doctorate.

1931   Rev. Clifford Gay
Rev. Clifford Gay entered Dr. Howell's Bible School, London to prepare for missionary service. Rev. Clifford Gay subsequently spent many years as a missionary in West Africa, mainly in the Cape Verde Islands.

Rev. Ivor Powell

1942   Rev. Jack Gardiner
Rev. Jack Gardiner was a Baptist Minister; he attended Spurgeon's College, London. He held a Baptist Ministry at Canterbury before moving to Southern Rhodesia (now Zimbabwe) and then South Africa.

Rev. and Mrs. Jack Gardiner.
In retirement Jack became Minister of Hermanus Church, South Africa.

1947   Rev. Ken Hibbs

Rev. Ken Hibbs, a member of Hope who had served in the RAF during WW II, entered Cardiff Baptist College to train for the Ministry. Rev. Ken Hibbs subsequently held pastorates at King Street, Abertillery and at Highbridge, Somerset before becoming a teacher of Religious Education in the Birmingham area.

Rev. Michael Thomas

Michael Thomas was the son of Mr. and Mrs. Clifford Thomas who were associated with Hope Church for many years. Bought up in Hope, Michael was particularly active in the Youth Group. A student of Pontywaun Grammar School it soon became clear that he would become an outstanding classics scholar; he entered King's College (University of London), in the early 1950s graduating with First Class Honours in Greek and Latin (circa 1954). He then entered the teaching profession and made outstanding progress to become Headmaster of Blundell's School (Dorset).

But Mrs. Thomas' great desire was that her son should enter the Baptist Ministry and this was fulfilled when, despite his eminently scholastic career, in mid-life, he decided to enter theological college.

He obtained the degree of Master of Theology from a theological college at Modesto (California) he then became Minister of the extremely lively Baptist congregation at East Sheen (nr. London. 01.06.1985). Mrs. Thomas passed away but Mr. Cliff Thomas, always an adherent at Hope, now decided to undergo baptism - at the age of 85!

Following his pastorate at East Sheen, Michael and his wife returned to the U.S.A; he was involved in a number of evangelical campaigns, including one in the Central American Republic of Guatemala. Michael and his wife then returned to this country. Very, very sadly, indeed, Michael passed away in 2005.

1998   David Leyshon

After serving as Pastor of Hope, failing health led David to give up this Ministry; David and his wife Debbie and their family moved in 1998 to the little Breton town of Belle Île En Terre. David's idea was to secure a base for Christian outreach in Brittany. A Christian Fellowship was established in Belle Île En Terre.

Maria Spencer's original intention was to serve as a missionary on the Ivory Coast (Africa); with this aim in mind she left Hope in 1987 to learn French at a French language school near Paris. However, plans changed. She met and married Emmanuel Hartiel, a French Christian, and after living and working near Paris for a few years, Maria and Emmanuel moved to join David Leyshon at Belle Île En Terre where a Christian cause had been established. Maria and Emmanuel were able to support David in his work; Emmanuel is now with David, joint leader in the ongoing Christian outreach in Belle Île En Terre.

1996-97   David Wilcox

David Wilcox, who had joined Hope from Moriah (Risca), was accepted for missionary work in Albania under the auspices of the Albanian Evangelical Mission.

In view of the unsettled state of Albania, David and his wife Pauline and family went first to Macedonia; Hope provided financial backing. Eventually they moved to Albania.

PART 3

HOPE SUNDAY SCHOOL BUILDING

This building at the rear of Hope Church was opened in 1933 as a Sunday School. It was originally the canteen erected to serve the temporary township for workers in the upper Grwyne Fawr Valley during the construction of the Black Mountains Reservoir (1913-1928). When this project was completed, the now surplus canteen building was purchased and relocated at the rear of Hope Church (this was a most commendable bit of initiative by the deacons at that time).

A further account is given in the article 'The Construction of the Grwyne Fawr Waterworks (1913-1928): A Relic at Crosskeys' by G.O. Osborne. This article appeared in *'Gwent Local History'*, Number 98, 2005, pp 63-8.

PART 4

THE CHURCH COVENANT AND STATEMENT OF FAITH

I BELIEVE IN GOD, THE FATHER, SON AND HOLY SPIRIT.

I BELIEVE IN THE LORD JESUS CHRIST, GOD'S SON AS MY PERSONAL SAVIOUR.

I BELIEVE THAT HE DIED ON THE CROSS AS MY SINBEARER, AND BECAUSE OF THIS I AM JUSTIFIED BY FAITH AND HAVE PEACE WITH GOD.

I BELIEVE THAT MY OWN SINFUL NATURE IS INCAPABLE OF A LIFE PLEASING TO GOD, BUT GOD IN HIS GREAT LOVE HAS GIVEN ME A NEW NATURE. THIS NEW NATURE IS MINE THROUGH FAITH IN CHRIST AND BY THE OPERATION OF THE HOLY SPIRIT I AM BORN AGAIN.

I BELIEVE THE BIBLE TO BE THE WORD OF GOD, WITHOUT ERROR IN THE ORIGINAL AND WHOLLY INSPIRED THROUGHOUT.

I TAKE IT AS MY RULE OF FAITH AND CONDUCT.

I PROMISE TO BE FAITHFUL AS FAR AS POSSIBLE IN ALL THE SERVICES OF THE CHURCH, TO READ MY BIBLE AND PRAY REGULARLY SO THAT I MAY GROW IN GRACE AND KNOWLEDGE OF THE LORD JESUS CHRIST.

I PROMISE TO SUPPORT THE WORK OF GOD WITH MY TALENTS, TIME AND MONETARY CONTRIBUTIONS, GIVING CHEERFULLY AND REGULARLY AS THE LORD PROSPERS ME.

I PROMISE TO BE CAREFUL IN KEEPING ALL BUSINESS MATTERS PERTAINING TO THE CHURCH WITHIN ITS CIRCLES AND NOT TO DISCUSS THEM WITH NON-MEMBERS.

I PROMISE TO GIVE AND RECEIVE ADVICE IN THE SPIRIT OF LOVE AND MEEKNESS, AND TO AVOID ALL CONTENTIONS AND STRIVINGS.

I ACCEPT THE DISCIPLINE OF THE CHURCH UNDER THE WORD OF GOD.

I HAVE CAREFULLY READ AND CONSIDERED THE COVENANT AND WHOLEHEARTEDLY ACCEPT IT AS A CONDITION OF MEMBERSHIP IN THE CHURCH.

TO THIS I MAKE MY PROMISE..........

Postscript

This is not the first history of Hope to be compiled. Records show that a brief history was compiled in 1930 for the church's Golden Jubilee celebrations. However, no trace of this publication remains and the present volume supplies a need. The history has, necessarily, been kept brief and, in the main, only salient events in the historical life of the church have been included. Naturally, most space is devoted to the earlier history of Hope; at these times there was more of historical significance to record. Regrettably, it has not been possible to include detailed histories of the Church Auxiliaries (Sunday School, Band of Hope, Sisterhood etc.) in this volume; this would have led to increased bulkiness, and arguably, might have somewhat upset the balance, since in these cases, due to lack of data, the earlier periods could not have been covered effectively.

From the facts on record in this volume a message emerges; appearing in the New International Version of the Bible and epitomised in Isaiah 51.1.

'Listen to me, you who pursue righteousness and who seek the LORD; Look to the rock from which you were cut and to the quarry from which you were hewn.'

Isaiah is here speaking to the Hebrews, now in captivity in Babylon. When he says *'Look to the rock from which you were cut'* what he means is *'Don't despair! Remember who you are! Remember God's covenant with you!'*

Today, some 2,500 years later on, in our vastly different society and times, these words are still relevant. So many people, far from feeling pride of ancestry, are, in fact, without any knowledge of the past and, of course, without thought for the future.

The contrast with the attitude of those who, during the last century, fought hard to establish Hope and hundreds of other churches, mainly Non-conformist, in south Wales is stark. The courage and tenacity of these pioneers is inspiring but, towering above these, the quality that really stands out is their enormous faith, i.e. their belief in and profession of the Gospel.

In these days of sometimes seemingly endless and often not very percipient debate, the true function of the Christian Church has often been the subject of long discussion. But the prime duty of the Church really is quite crystal clear; it is to preach the Gospel of Jesus Christ.

For our forbears this was the driving force behind the founding of Hope and the growth of Hope. The same force must sustain Hope as it moves through the second century of its existence.

References

Dates in brackets e.g. (2.2.98) refer to minutes of Church or Deacons' Meetings held at Hope.

(1)   Bassett T.M., 'The Welsh Baptists', Gomer Press; 1977, p13.

(2)   Rees T., 'History of Protestant Nonconformity in Wales', John Snow & Co.; 1883, pp90, 412.

(3)   Lewis H. Elvet, 'Nonconformity in Wales', Thomas Law, London; 1904, p17.

(4)   Davies E.T., 'Religion in the Industrial Revolution in South Wales', Univ. Wales Press; 1964, p84.